...for dustin.

Brenda has a beaver
and she's ready to confess...

...as soft and sweet as it may be
her beaver is a mess

Brenda's beaver's big
Brenda's beaver's hairy

Every guy who's seen it
    says that Brenda's beaver's scary

Brenda took her beaver
for a swim down at the lake

by the looks that she received
she figured that was a mistake

She stuffed that furry mound into a swimming suit

It stuck out all around...it was anything but cute

Some who saw it laughed...
...others were just stunned

Brenda's beaver was hanging out...
...soakin' up the sun

Her friends could not believe her
they said "We need to talk!"

They covered up her beaver
and they took her for a walk

"Brenda dear, listen here
we want to help you out...

Your beaver needs a makeover
...it really needs it now!"

"I hope we don't seem pushy"
said her biker friend named Kim

Savanna pulled her beaver back
to show off what she'd done

Hers has a nice long landing patch
it looks like it'd be fun

Krissy's beaver is quite rare
it could be worth a million

Hers is bare, it has no hair...her beaver is Brazilian

Catherine let her beaver loose
she said "There's nothin' to it...

Kim produced some scissors, and Krissy had some wax

Now all that Brenda had to do was sit back and relax

As they came towards her beaver,
they said "Now don't be scared...

...We're going to see what's underneath
that frumpy pile of hair!"

It ended in just minutes, they didn't leave her much

When Brenda's friends were finished
she and her beaver blushed

Her beaver was so tiny
they could not believe their eyes

It was smooth and it was shiny
...it was hard to recognize!

Now Brenda is so proud
it seems like every time we see her

She's in the center of a crowd
...just showing off her beaver